VIOLIN

101 CHRISTMAS SONGS

Available for
FLUTE, CLARINET, ALTO SAX, TENOR SAX, TRUMPET,
HORN, TROMBONE, VIOLIN, VIOLA, CELLO

ISBN 978-1-5400-3027-6

Visit Hal Leonard Online at
www.halleonard.com

Contact Us:
Hal Leonard
7777 West Bluemound Road
Milwaukee, WI 53213
Email: info@halleonard.com

In Europe contact:
Hal Leonard Europe Limited
42 Wigmore Street
Marylebone, London, W1U 2RN
Email: info@halleonardeurope.com

In Australia contact:
Hal Leonard Australia Pty. Ltd.
4 Lentara Court
Cheltenham, Victoria, 3192 Australia
Email: info@halleonard.com.au

CONTENTS

ALL I WANT FOR CHRISTMAS IS YOU

VIOLIN

Words and Music by MARIAH CAREY
and WALTER AFANASIEFF

ANGELS FROM THE REALMS OF GLORY

Words by JAMES MONTGOMERY
Music by HENRY T. SMART

Brightly

AS LONG AS THERE'S CHRISTMAS

from BEAUTY AND THE BEAST - THE ENCHANTED CHRISTMAS

VIOLIN

Music by RACHEL PORTMAN
Lyrics by DON BLACK

Moderately

AULD LANG SYNE

Words by ROBERT BURNS
Traditional Scottish Melody

ANGELS WE HAVE HEARD ON HIGH

Traditional French Carol

AWAY IN A MANGER

Music by JAMES R. MURRAY

Slowly

BABY, IT'S COLD OUTSIDE

VIOLIN

By FRANK LOESSER

Moderately

AWAY IN A MANGER

Music by JONATHAN E. SPILMAN

BECAUSE IT'S CHRISTMAS
(For All the Children)

Music by BARRY MANILOW
Lyric by BRUCE SUSSMAN and JACK FELDMAN

BELIEVE

from Warner Bros. Pictures' THE POLAR EXPRESS

VIOLIN

Words and Music by GLEN BALLARD
and ALAN SILVESTRI

Moderately slow

BLUE CHRISTMAS

Words and Music by BILLY HAYES
and JAY JOHNSON

With expression

BRAZILIAN SLEIGH BELLS

VIOLIN

By PERCY FAITH

To Coda ⊕

VIOLIN

CAROLING, CAROLING

Words by WIHLA HUTSON
Music by ALFRED BURT

THE BELLS OF ST. MARY'S

VIOLIN

Traditional
Words by DOUGLAS FURBER
Music by A. EMMETT ADAMS

Slowly, with freedom

A CHILD IS BORN

VIOLIN

By THAD JONES

THE CHIPMUNK SONG

Words and Music by
ROSS BAGDASARIAN

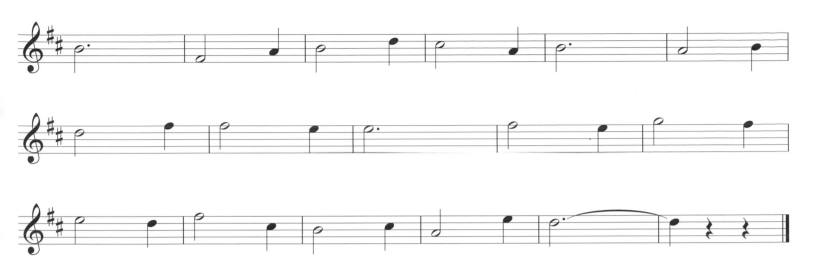

CHRISTMAS IN KILLARNEY

Words and Music by JOHN REDMOND
and FRANK WELDON

Moderately, with a lilt

VIOLIN

CHRISTMAS
(Baby Please Come Home)

Words and Music by PHIL SPECTOR,
ELLIE GREENWICH and JEFF BARRY

CHRISTMAS IS A-COMIN'
(May God Bless You)

VIOLIN

Words and Music by
FRANK LUTHER

Moderately slow

THE CHRISTMAS SONG
(Chestnuts Roasting on an Open Fire)

VIOLIN

Music and Lyric by MEL TORMÉ
and ROBERT WELLS

DO YOU WANT TO BUILD A SNOWMAN?

from FROZEN

VIOLIN

Music and Lyrics by KRISTEN ANDERSON-LOPEZ
and ROBERT LOPEZ

COLD DECEMBER NIGHT

VIOLIN

Words and Music by MICHAEL BUBLE,
ALAN CHANG and ROBERT ROCK

VIOLIN

CHRISTMAS TIME IS HERE
from A CHARLIE BROWN CHRISTMAS

Words by LEE MENDELSON
Music by VINCE GUARALDI

THE CHRISTMAS WALTZ

Words by SAMMY CAHN
Music by JULE STYNE

DANCE OF THE SUGAR PLUM FAIRY
from THE NUTCRACKER

By PYOTR IL'YICH TCHAIKOVSKY

DECK THE HALL

VIOLIN

Traditional Welsh Carol

Brightly

DO YOU HEAR WHAT I HEAR

Words and Music by NOEL REGNEY
and GLORIA SHAYNE

Moderately

THE FIRST NOEL

17th Century English Carol
Music from W. Sandys' *Christmas Carols*

FAIRYTALE OF NEW YORK

VIOLIN

Words and Music by JEREMY FINER
and SHANE MacGOWAN

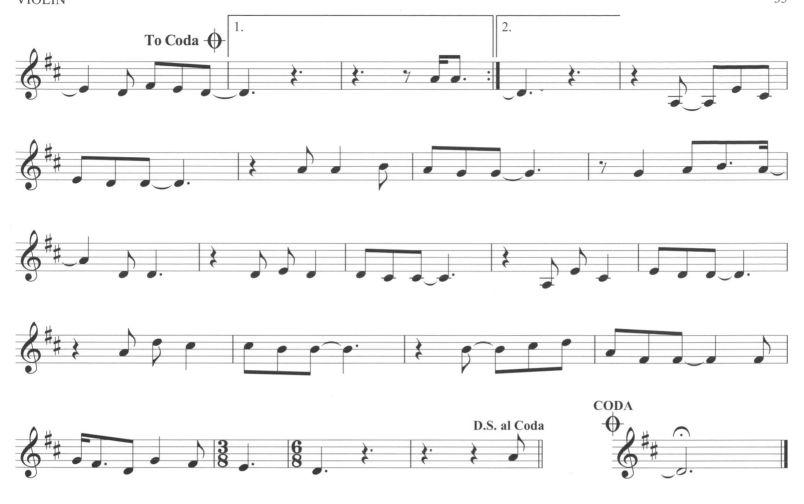

GOD REST YE MERRY, GENTLEMEN

Traditional English Carol

FELIZ NAVIDAD

VIOLIN

Music and Lyrics by
JOSÉ FELICIANO

GRANDMA GOT RUN OVER BY A REINDEER

VIOLIN

Words and Music by
RANDY BROOKS

THE GREATEST GIFT OF ALL

VIOLIN

Words and Music by
JOHN JARVIS

Moderately slow

GOOD KING WENCESLAS

Words by JOHN M. NEALE
Music from *Piae Cantiones*

Moderately

GROWN-UP CHRISTMAS LIST

VIOLIN

Words and Music by DAVID FOSTER
and LINDA THOMPSON-JENNER

Moderately slow

HARK! THE HERALD ANGELS SING

Words by CHARLES WESLEY
Music by FELIX MENDELSSOHN-BARTHOLDY

HAPPY XMAS
(War Is Over)

VIOLIN

Written by JOHN LENNON
and YOKO ONO

HAVE YOURSELF A MERRY LITTLE CHRISTMAS

from MEET ME IN ST. LOUIS

VIOLIN

Words and Music by HUGH MARTIN
and RALPH BLANE

Moderately slow

HAPPY HOLIDAY
from the Motion Picture Irving Berlin's HOLIDAY INN

Words and Music by
IRVING BERLIN

VIOLIN

HARD CANDY CHRISTMAS
from THE BEST LITTLE WHOREHOUSE IN TEXAS

Words and Music by
CAROL HALL

HERE COMES SANTA CLAUS
(Right Down Santa Claus Lane)

Words and Music by GENE AUTRY
and OAKLEY HALDEMAN

VIOLIN

(There's No Place Like)
HOME FOR THE HOLIDAYS

Words and Music by AL STILLMAN
and ROBERT ALLEN

I HEARD THE BELLS ON CHRISTMAS DAY

VIOLIN

Words by HENRY WADSWORTH LONGFELLOW
Music by JOHN BAPTISTE CALKIN

A HOLLY JOLLY CHRISTMAS

Music and Lyrics by
JOHNNY MARKS

I WANT A HIPPOPOTAMUS FOR CHRISTMAS
(Hippo the Hero)

VIOLIN

Words and Music by
JOHN ROX

I'LL BE HOME FOR CHRISTMAS

Words and Music by KIM GANNON
and WALTER KENT

Slowly

I HEARD THE BELLS ON CHRISTMAS DAY

VIOLIN

Words by HENRY WADSWORTH LONGFELLOW
Adapted by JOHNNY MARKS
Music by JOHNNY MARKS

Moderately

I SAW MOMMY KISSING SANTA CLAUS

Words and Music by
TOMMIE CONNOR

Moderately slow

I SAW THREE SHIPS

VIOLIN

Traditional English Carol

I WONDER AS I WANDER

By JOHN JACOB NILES

I'VE GOT MY LOVE TO KEEP ME WARM

from the 20th Century Fox Motion Picture ON THE AVENUE

VIOLIN

Words and Music by
IRVING BERLIN

Bright Jump tempo

IT'S BEGINNING TO LOOK LIKE CHRISTMAS

VIOLIN

By MEREDITH WILLSON

IT MUST HAVE BEEN THE MISTLETOE
(Our First Christmas)

VIOLIN

By JUSTIN WILDE
and DOUG KONECKY

IT CAME UPON THE MIDNIGHT CLEAR

Words by EDMUND H. SEARS
Traditional English Melody
Adapted by ARTHUR SULLIVAN

Moderately

JINGLE BELLS

VIOLIN

Words and Music by
J. PIERPONT

THE LAST MONTH OF THE YEAR
(What Month Was Jesus Born In?)

Words and Music by VERA HALL
Adapted and Arranged by RUBY PICKENS TARTT
and ALAN LOMAX

LET IT SNOW! LET IT SNOW! LET IT SNOW!

Words by SAMMY CAHN
Music by JULE STYNE

JOY TO THE WORLD

VIOLIN

Words by ISAAC WATTS
Music by GEORGE FRIDERIC HANDEL

Brightly

MARY'S LITTLE BOY CHILD

Words and Music by
JESTER HAIRSTON

Slowly and simply

LITTLE SAINT NICK

VIOLIN

Words and Music by BRIAN WILSON
and MIKE LOVE

MARCH OF THE TOYS

from BABES IN TOYLAND

VIOLIN

By VICTOR HERBERT

With spirit

A MARSHMALLOW WORLD

VIOLIN

Words by CARL SIGMAN
Music by PETER DE ROSE

MARY, DID YOU KNOW?

VIOLIN

Words and Music by MARK LOWRY
and BUDDY GREENE

MERRY CHRISTMAS, DARLING

VIOLIN

Words and Music by RICHARD CARPENTER
and FRANK POOLER

Freely

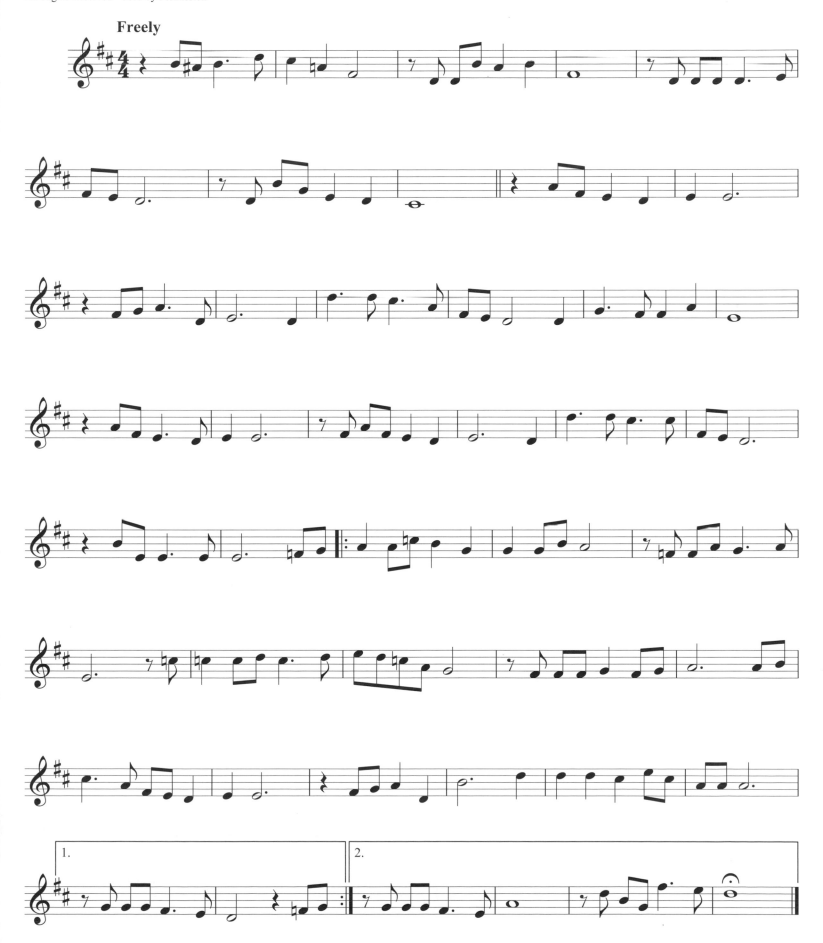

THE MOST WONDERFUL TIME OF THE YEAR

VIOLIN

Words and Music by EDDIE POLA
and GEORGE WYLE

MY FAVORITE THINGS
from THE SOUND OF MUSIC

Violin

Lyrics by OSCAR HAMMERSTEIN II
Music by RICHARD RODGERS

Lively

MELE KALIKIMAKA

VIOLIN

Words and Music by
R. ALEX ANDERSON

MISTER SANTA

Words and Music by
PAT BALLARD

MISTLETOE AND HOLLY

Words and Music by FRANK SINATRA,
DOK STANFORD and HENRY W. SANICOLA

O LITTLE TOWN OF BETHLEHEM

VIOLIN

Words by PHILLIPS BROOKS
Music by LEWIS H. REDNER

O HOLY NIGHT

French words by PLACIDE CAPPEAU
English words by JOHN S. DWIGHT
Music by ADOLPHE ADAM

SANTA CLAUS IS COMIN' TO TOWN

Words by HAVEN GILLESPIE
Music by J. FRED COOTS

O CHRISTMAS TREE

VIOLIN

Traditional German Carol

O COME, ALL YE FAITHFUL

Music by JOHN FRANCIS WADE

PARADE OF THE WOODEN SOLDIERS

VIOLIN

English Lyrics by BALLARD MacDONALD
Music by LEON JESSEL

PRETTY PAPER

VIOLIN

Words and Music by
WILLIE NELSON

ROCKIN' AROUND THE CHRISTMAS TREE

VIOLIN

Music and Lyrics by
JOHNNY MARKS

RUDOLPH THE RED-NOSED REINDEER

VIOLIN

Music and Lyrics by
JOHNNY MARKS

SANTA BABY

VIOLIN

By JOAN JAVITS,
PHIL SPRINGER and TONY SPRINGER

SHAKE ME I RATTLE
(Squeeze Me I Cry)

VIOLIN

Words and Music by HAL HACKADY
and CHARLES NAYLOR

Moderately slow

SILVER AND GOLD

Music and Lyrics by
JOHNNY MARKS

Slowly and expressively

SILVER BELLS

from the Paramount Picture THE LEMON DROP KID

Words and Music by JAY LIVINGSTON
and RAY EVANS

Moderately

THAT'S CHRISTMAS TO ME

VIOLIN

Words and Music by KEVIN OLUSOLA
and SCOTT HOYING

Moderately

SILENT NIGHT

VIOLIN

Words by JOSEPH MOHR
Translated by JOHN F. YOUNG
Music by FRANZ X. GRUBER

SING WE NOW OF CHRISTMAS

Traditional French Carol

SOMEWHERE IN MY MEMORY
from the Twentieth Century Fox Motion Picture HOME ALONE

VIOLIN

Words by LESLIE BRICUSSE
Music by JOHN WILLIAMS

Gently and with simplicity

THE STAR CAROL

Lyric by WIHLA HUTSON
Music by ALFRED BURT

Tenderly, with much expression

THIS CHRISTMAS

VIOLIN

Words and Music by DONNY HATHAWAY
and NADINE McKINNOR

TOYLAND
from BABES IN TOYLAND

VIOLIN

Words by GLEN MacDONOUGH
Music by VICTOR HERBERT

Slowly

UP ON THE HOUSETOP

Words and Music by
B.R. HANBY

Brightly

WE NEED A LITTLE CHRISTMAS
from MAME

VIOLIN

Music and Lyric by
JERRY HERMAN

THE TWELVE DAYS OF CHRISTMAS

VIOLIN

Traditional English Carol

Moderately
Verse 1

Verses 2-4

Verse 5

Verses 6-12

*These bars are played a different number of times for each verse.

WE WISH YOU THE MERRIEST

VIOLIN

Words and Music by
LES BROWN

WE THREE KINGS OF ORIENT ARE

VIOLIN

Words and Music by
JOHN H. HOPKINS, JR.

WE WISH YOU A MERRY CHRISTMAS

Traditional English Folksong

WHAT ARE YOU DOING NEW YEAR'S EVE?

VIOLIN

By FRANK LOESSER

Slowly and sentimentally

WONDERFUL CHRISTMASTIME

VIOLIN

Words and Music by
PAUL McCARTNEY

Brightly

WHAT CHILD IS THIS?

VIOLIN

Words by WILLIAM C. DIX
16th Century English Melody

Moderately slow

WHITE CHRISTMAS
from the Motion Picture Irving Berlin's HOLIDAY INN

Words and Music by
IRVING BERLIN

Slowly, in 2

YOU'RE ALL I WANT FOR CHRISTMAS

Words and Music by GLEN MOORE
and SEGER ELLIS

Slowly and evenly

THE WONDERFUL WORLD OF CHRISTMAS

VIOLIN

Words by CHARLES TOBIAS
Music by AL FRISCH

101 SONGS

BIG COLLECTIONS OF FAVORITE SONGS ARRANGED FOR SOLO INSTRUMENTALISTS.

101 BROADWAY SONGS

00154199 Flute	$15.99
00154200 Clarinet	$15.99
00154201 Alto Sax	$15.99
00154202 Tenor Sax	$16.99
00154203 Trumpet	$15.99
00154204 Horn	$15.99
00154205 Trombone	$15.99
00154206 Violin	$15.99
00154207 Viola	$15.99
00154208 Cello	$15.99

101 DISNEY SONGS

00244104 Flute	$17.99
00244106 Clarinet	$17.99
00244107 Alto Sax	$17.99
00244108 Tenor Sax	$17.99
00244109 Trumpet	$17.99
00244112 Horn	$17.99
00244120 Trombone	$17.99
00244121 Violin	$17.99
00244125 Viola	$17.99
00244126 Cello	$17.99

101 MOVIE HITS

00158087 Flute	$15.99
00158088 Clarinet	$15.99
00158089 Alto Sax	$15.99
00158090 Tenor Sax	$15.99
00158091 Trumpet	$15.99
00158092 Horn	$15.99
00158093 Trombone	$15.99
00158094 Violin	$15.99
00158095 Viola	$15.99
00158096 Cello	$15.99

101 CHRISTMAS SONGS

00278637 Flute	$15.99
00278638 Clarinet	$15.99
00278639 Alto Sax	$15.99
00278640 Tenor Sax	$15.99
00278641 Trumpet	$15.99
00278642 Horn	$14.99
00278643 Trombone	$15.99
00278644 Violin	$15.99
00278645 Viola	$15.99
00278646 Cello	$15.99

101 HIT SONGS

00194561 Flute	$17.99
00197182 Clarinet	$17.99
00197183 Alto Sax	$17.99
00197184 Tenor Sax	$17.99
00197185 Trumpet	$17.99
00197186 Horn	$17.99
00197187 Trombone	$17.99
00197188 Violin	$17.99
00197189 Viola	$17.99
00197190 Cello	$17.99

101 POPULAR SONGS

00224722 Flute	$17.99
00224723 Clarinet	$17.99
00224724 Alto Sax	$17.99
00224725 Tenor Sax	$17.99
00224726 Trumpet	$17.99
00224727 Horn	$17.99
00224728 Trombone	$17.99
00224729 Violin	$17.99
00224730 Viola	$17.99
00224731 Cello	$17.99

101 CLASSICAL THEMES

00155315 Flute	$15.99
00155317 Clarinet	$15.99
00155318 Alto Sax	$15.99
00155319 Tenor Sax	$15.99
00155320 Trumpet	$15.99
00155321 Horn	$15.99
00155322 Trombone	$15.99
00155323 Violin	$15.99
00155324 Viola	$15.99
00155325 Cello	$15.99

101 JAZZ SONGS

00146363 Flute	$15.99
00146364 Clarinet	$15.99
00146366 Alto Sax	$15.99
00146367 Tenor Sax	$15.99
00146368 Trumpet	$15.99
00146369 Horn	$14.99
00146370 Trombone	$15.99
00146371 Violin	$15.99
00146372 Viola	$15.99
00146373 Cello	$15.99

101 MOST BEAUTIFUL SONGS

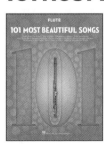

00291023 Flute	$16.99
00291041 Clarinet	$16.99
00291042 Alto Sax	$17.99
00291043 Tenor Sax	$17.99
00291044 Trumpet	$16.99
00291045 Horn	$16.99
00291046 Trombone	$16.99
00291047 Violin	$16.99
00291048 Viola	$16.99
00291049 Cello	$17.99

See complete song lists and sample pages at www.halleonard.com

0222

Prices, contents and availability subject to change without notice.